**Just
Because**
Neetha Kunaratnam

STACK
BOOKS

Smokestack Books
1 Lake Terrace, Grewelthorpe, Ripon HG4 3BU
e-mail: info@smokestack-books.co.uk
www.smokestack-books.co.uk

ISBN 9781999827694

Smokestack Books
is represented
by Inpress Ltd

**Just
Because**

*For Emma, Amber and Lara.
In honour of my parents,
75 and 80 this year.*

Contents

from the frontline

We ran, and the planes grazed our hair,
And then they were no more
As we stood dazed in the burning city,
But, of course, they didn't film that.
Charles Simic

The Afterlife

After every war
someone has to clean up. Things won't
straighten themselves up, after all
Wislava Szymborska, *The End and the Beginning*

And someone will have to clean up,
but this is no job for ordinary Joes,
only specialists padded in moon boots,
face masks, and white chemical suits,

so someone will have to write a cheque
for the foreign input, the expertise
and expensive equipment:
the mine detectors and nerve sensors.

Somebody will need to order them
from the catalogue, ignore the new
solar-powered, GPS models, choose
the standard, remote-controlled breed,

as faithful and expendable as someone
sought to cordon off the area, skirt the perimeters
on tiptoe, mark out the dimensions
of the operation with sniffer dogs in tow.

Someone will need to believe the aggrieved
can make a difference, pray in numbers, petition
our leaders to subsidize farmers who can no
longer reap lest they're blown into thin air...

Someone will have to locate, then collect
any bright packages dropped after
the bombers droned off into the night,
their black boxes still replaying screams,

and someone sort out the dried food
from the prosthetic limbs, filter out the notes
of explanation, decipher a rationale
from the mistakes made in translation.

Someone will have to point out
that mustard leaves might not survive the blasts,
and checking they've turned red might set off
a barrage of blinding and a cluster of regrets.

Somebody will have to teach the children
that these M&Ms aren't filled with peanuts
but pack an almighty punch. Explain that
a bomb as small as a battery can turn a sheep into a cloud.

Curfew

Sri Lanka, August 1983

The red betel smeared on our jowls was meant
to cure our mumps, but made us conspicuous,

so at every checkpoint we were told to reiterate
burgher caste, in spite of our dark Tamil skin,

being too young to be entrusted with the proof
of our British passports. Buying provisions had by then

become a treacherous task, and the tension in the house
only eased if everyone was home by dusk. Then the

gunshots would start up, announcing the curfew, and repeat
at regular intervals, like whips cracking ominously up the street,

until you could sense them knocking at the door.
Then one evening, unannounced, mum hissed that

the storm troopers were coming, to quickly get dressed.
(later, she would tell us Darth Vader was Singhalese,

but by then no analogy would suffice.) We rushed into the cellar,
eyes pounding, a nickel stink corroded our shallow breathing,

and we hid, wheezing, until the footsteps had disappeared
overhead, and the gunshots been wrung out of earshot.

Carted out of town the next day, in an open-topped van, we reached
the refugee camp, makeshift like a school turned polling station,

and took sanctuary a few nights. Huddled on the floor in blankets,
a dark ocean of bodies and familial territories, children spied

at each other curiously, before learning slowly to dim the glare,
improvise, share: brush our teeth with *Thambi's* mint leaves,

enjoy the neighbours' chai, with its excess of cardamom,
dish out the boiled sweets though no one was car sick,

until one time I woke up forgetting- a seven year old again,
so selfish and intractable that, not knowing she had gone for water,

I tearfully reproached my cousin
for borrowing my sandals and not bringing them back in time.

Front Page

the third take

clinched the photo-op,
the flashbulb whooshed
as euphoric men
on a hill of gorse
planted their emblem
into sulphurous ash

the third take

pleases the committee
who deem the men's
jaw-lines worthy,
in their words:
haggard, salt-
patched and gaunt

the third take

will trundle in mass copy:
the sun stream behind
the star-striped flutter,
and warriors sloped
under the pole, their
six packs clenched.

Protest

The delegates in Teflon suits emerge from the vacuum
of the plush conference room,
and sip and schmooze in the theatre's spacious foyer.

Over coffee and cake, they digest tech spec,
dissect the briefing
on infrared homing, and the hand-held footage

of two run-throughs, filmed *Blair-Witch-style* in the dust
of Falluja and Kabul.
Price lists are consulted, emails pinged to HQ.

For this matinee stand-off, we assemble in protest,
a rag-tag cast of fifty
hogging the back lawns, with banners demanding

Arms Dealers Out! Thinktank think! Weapons Smart!

Jeering from the wings, we presume the police cordon
is part of the performance:
truncheons brandished to dissuade hecklers,

their bolshy frowns impassive to our one-liners,
their bullet-proof vests
an extravagance to repel our djembe beats.

Then from the glass balcony of the hospitality suite,
one bullish antagonist
flashes us a gloating grin, drawing a gasp as he cups

his hand to his ear, mouthing – *I can't fucking hear you*,

and I lose it in a volley of abuse, feeling so incandescent
that the expletives soothe me,
until an officer, luminous in his reflective apparel, deadpans:

'Please Sir, there are *children* with you.'

Poppy

You see it can be undone,
rather than torn.
So we pick it apart
to see its four forms.

Its petal is an
overlap of lungs,
a radii of ridges
that my thumbs caress.

Its shard of leaf
is a disfigured hand,
frostbitten knuckles
numbed by shrapnel.

The plastic needle
gently pricks me.
Its sawn-off stem
slips in like a spine,

and latches on the collar
of the cotyledon.
The black button
that locks it all

is the perfect disc
of an exit wound,
a pupil dilated in
its bloodshot eye.

Raid

The residual heat in the velux frames
has enticed a hundred flies to nestle
like indelible Velcro beads.

Peering in, inky blobs tumble out
with a motorised hum. Some rebound
or splutter back up,

and I see the bristly tar sliding
its molten coat along
the pine ledges and underfelt.

To air the room completely may mean
my flailing dishcloth arm
is enveloped by their treacle,

which might spread to the flashings,
fill the gutter, and breed so fast
that this sleek can of Raid seems a cure.

As the drowsy throng tucks in,
I line the tufted cream carpet
with yellowing tabloids,

knowing the carnage may resemble
a writhing of full stops.
I exhale, poised for the dark to spill,

hoping, once I've hoovered,
that the stale air might once more
appear fresh and forgiving.

Paintballing

I am chaperone for these games,
this friendly fire with tea breaks thrown in;
I hadn't really planned to watch,
but my eyes sharpen like snipers

at the sniff of dried sweat on deadened skin;
embedded, I am a tick burrowing to the core,
third party to these mini massacres,
implicated in the hard shit
that comes with the warfare.

Having chosen not to play, I am *neutralized*,
so observe from the *Dead Zone*, a cage
with grandstand view and protective netting
to stem these automatic experiments

of some fifty acolytes of Pollock,
masked anonymously like storm-troopers
whose tactics have been scuppered
by adrenaline. *Why don't you play*,
they keep asking, and mishearing,

I wonder what prayer
has to do with anything,
when their lungs are spent
like uzis, and their faces blood-drawn.

Nine Die in Suicide Bombing

Eleven if you include the bomber
herself, and the moulting grey canine.

Four died oblivious, their minds combusted,
but six had considered their own mortality

that very day, of whom four had prayed and two toyed,
for reasons unknown, with the idea of self-immolation.

The stats of divine vengeance were: three Catholic, three Agnostic
and three Muslim. There was one Other, Miss X, and the Alsatian.

Three were stood on the platform,
five were running late and the dog was asleep

with the tramp, Mr Z, when fire stopped the clock.
14:26 was the official time of death but two

watches were slow and three fast. Two were
drenched in coats and five in suits, although the

rain had long since given way to sunshine.
Five were still carrying umbrellas, which maimed them.

Half of the victims hailed from the soil and half the concrete.
Spores of fear crackled in the air, electrifying

all fifty-six witnesses, the majority of whom
sustained serious injury, and echoed the explosion

with fearsome cries. Most were traumatized,
even those who had been caught daydreaming.

Three Cemeteries, Normandy

German Cemetery, La Cambe

The headstones cast
their geometry of
succinct shadows,
and severed phlox
perfumes the air
where lawn tractors
have mown y-axes
of gradated green.

Morning and dusk, sprinklers feed the limpid comb-over
that covers the cracked earth

and each tomb
is a co-ordinate of loss
in this matrix of deaths,
placed in parallel
on its own asymptote.
Even in the shared graves
it feels as if
no sorrows overlap.

Commonwealth War Cemetery, Bayeux

In the quiet season
a lone mower trundles
in the drizzle.
Its motorised hum
breaks the leafy hush,
blotting out
the gruff voice
of a schoolboy reciting
authorized poetry.

It stops mid-way as experts in overalls and gas masks

remove lichen
from the headstones,
and remove the scrawl
of defiant graffiti
with a product that
makes the nostrils rasp,
and the skin of the air
moult, and the bees
falter in mid-flight.

Vierville-sur-mer

The beach is scarred,
as if sea salt has
healed the sand,
and trails of pus
coagulate in the tide's
foaming return.
Marram bristles
as seagulls sweep in
to shit on the strand,

where carefree hands have etched their name
Back up the incline, tombs dot the hill

like pale collateral
and flagpoles have
churned up the mud.
O vast sea of green:
dream the sutured
crosses gone,
their swell of scars
picked clean from
the skin graft of the lawn.

live now
to London

*(given the scalpel, they dissect a kiss;
or, sold the reason, they undream a dream)*
e e cummings

Refuse

The garbage men are on strike.
In our lane, bulbous bin bags
have burst their waistlines,
scavengers to blame perhaps,
but now a dark effervescence of flies

clouds the trail, shape-shifts
over spat-up rags of chicken,
charred gristle and bones,
laps up half-priced houmous
long past the sell-by date.

Tip-toeing through the filth
and forgotten flyers, kicking
a path past polystyrene, I see
a crowd gather to watch,
dogs taut under the leash,

wonder if this vixen splayed
on the kerb heard the bugle
of brakes, as two officers wrap
its corpse in a ripped bin bag
that's black as a shotgun.

Confrontation

I stride behind
these bad, brawny youths,
four coarse wannabes
lurching their macho bulk
under the centrifugal sun,
scattering verbal fire
in this High Street
High Noon showdown

***

Coke cans and cobblestones
as I avoid their eyes.
Wolf whistles wind me,
knock out my stuffing,
leaving this chicken self,
with goose bumps arising
from the breeze's
bold collusion

***

The klaxon and slipstream
of the departing bus
leave me puckering for air,
spewing for respite
from their two-fingered
vilification, and fists
admonishing me from
the back row smokescreen

Closed Circuit

They said I could stare
to my heart's content.
The thrill of a ringside seat,
plus cash up front to sit in
the van and kick back for

Saturday night: a line-up
of hair-pulling, meaty
fists thumping, the
jagged grin of broken
bottles and knives.

The action's so thick
and fast, I'm often out
of sync, and can't make
out the blood stain
in the sulphur light.

Only the timer on screen
keeps up with my pulse.
There's always slapstick
to calm me a notch:
a bloke in a mac who

steals from a drunken girl,
ducks down the alley
like Benny Hill, her friends
in hot pursuit: minis twitching,
heels tripping, boob tubes up in arms.

Sometimes I lose myself
in all twenty screens;
My brain's so full of limbo,
I don't know what's live
and what's a repeat.

Six months of this shit
and my senses are shot;
I dream of dust-ups
and awake to black,
but no closing credits roll.

Doggerel

They meet
for the first time
under the streetlamp,
set back from this
car park, yards
from an intersection.

They greet in gloves,
a few key words
set the mood,
a nip of the hipflask
raises it a notch,
then they flaunt
their hammered bodies
at a surveillance camera.

A nodding nightwatchman
sees dark urges
long withheld,
coming a-cropper
on bushes and railings,
broadband strangers
thrillingly undressed
in tickling cross-winds.

In the pleat of cold night
air, fingers buckle and mouths
creak for a sense of within.

Kitchen Sunk

Mascara smeared her melodrama,
drying Chablis stunning her lips
with a quiet confession that

she thirty-seven, he just eighteen,
was a match made in heaven.
Her husband's heaving hands,

rough and bruising, had convinced
her of a neighbour's touch,
but a boy's soft consolation

was what she got. She hung
her bait on naughty texts,
freed up a window for late lunches

to manoeuvre him into positions
he took on with relish.
His preference was nudity

and post-coital cigarettes, so they
did it at the kitchen table, or standing up,
always before coffee and the washing up,

until she tired of the novelty, spiced it
with monologue: taboo-strewn smut
that made him cringe impossibly.

The appliances murmured apologies,
as her jewelled knuckles impressed
upon him a desperate education.

Hatred has a shelf life, she told herself
later, preparing the lamb shank with
shredded sorrel, lovage and sage.

Boy, Man, Machine

In the platform's unbearable heat,
the boy wails at a vending machine,
prods his mother with stubborn fist,

seeking behind the glass partition
the bottles' latent fizz. Slaps down
at the keypad with block digits.

To which she seethes *shut it,*
so the boy wires up his voice-
box to the max, and points

and screams, craving the coin
that will get him his fix. *That's enough*
yells the mother, dragging him away.

We watch a man offer money to
the machine for a drink. The penny drops
but the lever jams, glinting in apology.

The machine entrances penniless boys
with a sunshine wink. Its only concession
a number to call for complaints.

Night Watch

Our paths crossed only once,
that rainy Monday of the tube strike.
Otherwise I would never have had
the pleasure of his scar and tell
anecdotes, the cut and thrust
of when he was held at gunpoint,
the three times he got knifed,
the stitches on his face and ribcage.

Sensing he had said too much,
me a beginner and all,
he told me not to worry,
no one wanted to intrude on these
luxury apartments they were doing up.
Squatters didn't carry knives and
I was *opposite the police station*
for Christ's sake. Great Portland Street,
not effing Brixton.

I left him to it, smarting.
He wasn't to know
I was unused to
sleeping on my feet,
that I was still overcoming
the unexpected visitations
of the previous night:

the cats fighting
over the tarpaulin,
scratching their claws
into the scaffolding

and the rasta painter
kicking his way past them,
back from the nightclub shift,
where he had cheated on
his wife with two Russian blondes,

telling me to let him work in peace,
pinning me to the wall
with his hatred, eyes and fist,

the dope coating my lungs black,
the white paint of his dreadlocks
recalling an angered, voodoo spirit.

Christmas Eve

Snow soundproofs the emptied street.
The wheezing stranger siphons
cash from the machine.

Its beeped thanks
of transaction punctures
the cloistered scene,

as he enters the shop
to buy up surplus stock
of luxury crackers and ham.

His white beard
is a festive disguise,
according him free rein

to rummage the car park bins
for withered sprouts, pigs in
blankets, and mince pies.

His sludge-spun car
revs its charred complaint
to no avail. He's stranded

until goodwill prevails
and three passing men heave
to set it straight.

With cautious traction
he heads for the food bank
to share his rotten spoils.

Tomorrow Never Knows

December 2006

Snug in the slipstream of this peloton of passengers
I trundle through the turnstiles,
tighten my headphones,
twist the wheel under my iPod's cracked screen,
and decipher a mood
for the journey underground.

I tune into a psychedelic cocoon –
it's the Beatles' *Tomorrow Never Knows*,
which puts a spring in my step,
as the high-hat syncopates
over the tambura drone,
and reversed guitars scramble loops
over cartwheels of buoyant bass.

On my way to the Tube,
my eyes lock onto scattered clusters
of singular bodies
that sashay and polka,
mulling as they merengue,
reflective as they rumba,
but never quite in sync.

Nanograms of data vibrate
in private soundscapes,
in rhythms that metabolise the dancers
whose soles rebound with oomph
on the cracked marble tiling.

I feel misaligned in this flash mob, caught
between exhibition and discretion,
as if I've stumbled upon a mating ritual
exclusive to telepaths,
so I rip the wire out of the jack,

and in the suddenly muted ambiance,
these mime artists uncoil robotic limbs,
and glumly bend their rusty knees,
until my ears make out the tannoy system
apologise for delays.

Sobered by this staccato,
I lock back into my collage of sonic pulses
from 1966, where eight-track seagulls squawk
and mocking ivories mimic an ice-cream van,

and I know this soundtrack
might be mine alone this December evening
as I venture on into London's belly

with the song's mantra insisting:
of the beginning, of the beginning, of the beginning,
until the battery fades in the tunnel
somewhere past Holborn.

just because

Et c'est assez, pour le poète,
d'être la mauvaise conscience
de son temps.
Saint-John Perse

Doomsday

From nowhere,
in the washing machine's drum:
doubloons, shillings and a small black crucifix.

In the mailbox, a postcard from Antarctica
sent by an ex, *the nightlife's wild,*
the sunshine's great, wish you were here,

and a blackmail note, with photographic proof,
from the fantasy muse upon whom
you had never laid a hand.

On the answering machine, a wrong number:
a woman confesses sins,
coughs up tears like sputum, hangs up,

while on TV, a sacrificial cult
attains glory in the name of a guy
with whom you once packed boxes.

On the train back to where you were born,
a man says he dreamt this very meeting,
knows your credit history and mother's maiden name:

then, re-entering the city to see her,
past the emptied cars and blinking lights,
and litter's eerie rustle on shop fronts

there are cats squealing shanties,
magpies smashing windscreens,
and a crow eyeing your front door.

Inquest

The coroner's report added much
to the mystery of her passing, and did little
to spotlight its causes, proving unable to pinpoint
any change in the girl's metabolism during
the period of her disappearance which,
the police surmised, *she spent camped out*
in bus shelters and warehouses.

The investigation's main source of inquiry
was the girl's mobile phone, not so much for
the call log of a thousand unanswered and
two made, (*to a Pizza Delivery, and a*
help-line), but the video footage,
photos and draft texts that *served as diary*
if correctly pieced together.

The entries suggested she stuck to five
daily fruit, although there was the odd
pronouncement berating love, berating loss.
She prefaced each video with title,
time and place but most were
litter blowing in alleys,
gulls swooping over landfill.

The photos proved *symptomatic*
of no overriding state of mind, showing
instead the gamut of emotions she endured:
the cracked, ventriloquist's smile,
the death stare, her goofy giggles,
her most sardonic eyebrow
in every shade of contempt

she could muster, all offset
by the same brick background,
the same red and beige boxes,
scuppering all attempts to conclude
*she had suffered jealousy and a broken
heart,* or record the official cause
of death as misadventure.

Airmail

When the co-pilot
locates the problem,
he radios for help,
then promptly rushes
back to the cargo
to scatter
as much of
it as he can into
the cornfields, lying
neat and golden
underneath their
flight path.

By then,
the engine
fire has already
spread
to the bags
and parcels, so
before the villagers even
hear the crash or
see the wreckage,
those who have been
sky-watching
are taken aback by
the portent of
someone's mail
tumbling to earth,
like snow flakes
that have grazed a
comet and are
curling up in
gravity's pull…

Guru Sat Nav

Cross-legged in saffron robes,
he opens his eyes to

incensed smoke, incants
his long-held decision

that *you're on your own*,
wishes you godspeed

and steady rhythm, trusting
you'll know when to

shut off the engine
and freewheel.

Popeye Comes Clean

I cansht standsh no more, I tellsh yer,
I haz to tellsh the truthsk: it wuzh all aboutsk
a deshkimal point. Spinashk ainsht

as ferroushk as you migsht thinksk,
dough the cansh presherve some nootshrientsk.
Didn'tsht yer ever sushpectsk

the producksh placshkment?
Didn'tsht it sheem odd
I alwayshk had a can up me schleeve?

Didsht yer relly shink I likshked der tashte
of alumniumshk on me tung?
God, I misshed der freshk shtuff

but it alwaysh tickld me gud I made
shpokeshman for der indusththree wid
my blindshk eye, speechsk impedimentshk

an not bein vegskitarian.
But I never onshe complaind
I sher as hell knew me playsh-

I wuzh but Ham Gravyshk
whippin boy bfur dey shpotted
de futskure wuzh in canned vej.

I do wantsht to lay some ghostsh
to restsk about Bluto and meshelf, yesh
we *wer* an iterm durin our shailor dayz:

Goin off to bootsh the Natshkeesh and de Japz
relly brung ush closhe, and de resht wuz
Yankee Doodle and toot toot,

dough the timez wer crool so we kept it shtum
and it fizzkled out, but blow me if we
didnsht just bout manij ter shtay frendsh.

Here in de retirementshk home, I playz
bingo all me howerz long, boozhin
shumtime on wheatgrassh wid Bettsky Boop,

laffin bout de olden dayz in Thimble
Theatrsk, wundrin how de publiksh fell hooksh,
lines an shinker for me charmzk. Me honeshty

I guesshk, that etrnel trooshk on
me graveshtone: 'I yam wht I yam,
and dat's all dat I yam.'

Family History

Staring down the sight
of her sawn-off .22
she saw the pigs
squelch and snout
into the water trough,

her grammy
on the porch, rocking
in and out of herself,
quirting like
a whip-poor-will.

Billy spying back
at her from
under his hat,
toting 10 cent blades
to stem his whiskers.

Her grampa shooting
bottles off the wall,
pinging scales of glass,
grunting at
ricochets of stone.

Her ma,
who told her
never catch the eye
of strangers, specially
no plantation boys.

Whom they took
away for five years
for shooting the after-
noon into smithereens,
who returned

in fury as
ashen as moonlight,
to brand swastikas
into every pig's
flank and haunches.

Libertine

I'd always thought myself
open-minded, tolerant
of everyone's right to love:
held men's hands in India,
kissed their cheeks in Provence.
Fuelled by a liqueur's magic,
I even let my tongue slip in,
and once, with my wife's consent,
let another man swallow me whole.

Yet, I'll admit I squirmed
in my seat when our son
brought his latest home.
Please don't get me wrong:
he seems so taken with Jerome.
Hell, the boy might even be the *one*.
But something about
the mechanics of it all
makes me queasy.

That night I asked
my wife how it feels
to have someone inside you,
to love them enough
they swell and contract
about the sphincter.
Once you let them in,
does it break you open,
or stopper you up?

Singin' in the Rain

Stinkin' of 'flu, Gene Kelly
taps and tuts in his trailer.
Raging with a fever of 103,
he wants to smoke, but thinks better
of it, and storms out to have a pop
at the group of cigared men
who want to spike the raindrops
with milk, so they'll show up in

glorious Technicolor.
Anger gives him wings. Het
up like a banshee, he hollers
as if struck by lightning,
taps out of his sodden skin,
slumps, smiling, in a heap of sweat.

The Courting of Silhouette Artists

They meet as fists, uptight at first,
before breaking into handshakes.
Then the parting of fingers brings
about a smile, the intimation
of a kiss, a promise of cuticles.

A mating ritual is a performance
so overpowering you wouldn't
want to intrude. The hares' ears
show mutual interest and
a fond keenness, before crouching

down into frogs' mouths,
ready to coalesce if they come close,
or one decides to extend himself,
and the other to bite down
and swallow him up, but this

would require a role-play of submission;
they might decide instead to start
on an equal footing, forming a butterfly,
a gorgon's head, or two Venus flytraps,
lock-jawed and pulsing.

Train Scene

As the troll-eyed fellow
trundled to the bar,
swaying in the aisle,

the rest of the carriage
returned to their books,
and let out a collective sigh,

stunned that he had yelled
I'm Spartacus,
and expected them to reply.

Between the Lines

As for colouring books,
you never really liked
to stay within the lines,
so skin merged into clothes
and lipstick bled from mouths.

You favoured dot-to-dots,
divining skeletal structures
in surfaces, wanting
to 2B your way along
the skirting and architraves.

At tea, your mother's guests
gossiped or talked shop.
Left, then, to your own devices,
you scoured drawers
and drew inferences from points

where angles converged:
dusty corners, hinges.
That day you struck the jackpot,
a dot-to-dot in her wardrobe
that your father had gifted her

one Valentine. With careful,
tongue-poking accuracy,
you laboured at the new forms,
the connecting centrepiece so bold
that you were moved to shade it in.

Satisfaction seeking praise,
you scampered down banisters,
brandishing the completed page,
so mother and her frozen clique
could give it the once over.

For years you'd recall
the blood rush as you raced
to your room, frowns topping smirks,
the manners of mirth, *doggy style*
a phrase learnt with a snigger.

Tony Bear

… honey-pot despot
writes His life up
on a gilt-edged desktop,
casts Himself as
a youthful sexpot,
with spindly hair
as taut as the cat gut
on his tennis-racket-
air-guitar-Apollo's-lyre.

Curating his legacy,
he does not detail,
so much as footnote
those hot-to-trot
foreign affairs
in which he dabbled,
driven on by *God-
-only-knows-what*
tin-pot libido.

Eyes bloodshot
like a hounded fox,
he cannot stop
as the deadline nears
when he can soapbox
at the book launch of
The Divine Plot:
The Life and Times of
a right-minded Bear.

A Murder of Crows...

A pity of pine forests
A muddle of strategists
A gleam of lawsuits
A back-track of economists

A pittance of philanthropists
A bling of retail therapists
A nut-rub of shoppers
A sulk of cashiers

A cufflink of Henrys
A hurrah of haberdashers
A fidget of lovers
A filigree of fetishists

A muster of matriarchs
A strap-on of oligarchs
A hush-hush of committees
A skid mark of scandals

A fistful of footballers
A studs-up of politicians
A sadness of soldiers
A plunder of paparazzi

A slugfest of screenplays
A rumble of Mafiosi
A joust of bloggers
A callus of critics

A geddit of comics
An ugh of urbanites
An exhaustion of metaphors
A bamboozle of etceteras

Bystanders

Presenting to the class,
my quietest student asks
how we'd react
if we saw a stranger
bleed out in the street.

Her sequence of slides
on the *bystander effect*
claims we won't stop,
trusting paramedics
to get there in time,

a first-aider to surge
from the crowd
and tourniquet with rags,
or a passing priest
to observe the last rites.

Her voice bristles
as she tells us of
the culture in which
to mind one's business
is to turn one's back.

There are no questions
in the pensive room,
as we watch the footage
one more time:
the van knocking over

the child, the eighteen
witnesses ghosting by,
the car that snaps her frame,
and the exhaust fumes
that linger in its wake.

Strike

For forty days
I have abstained
from solids.

Only water has
passed through me
like a daily rain,

a sort of ablution
to stave off
fatal rust.

I can barely
reach the sink
to clean my teeth,

ma complains
of my bad breath
and I see myself

shrink in her
shallow eyes.
But I can't give up,

it's too late
to retract; I know
I won't get up

again: my knee
sockets are too
heavy for my legs,

and my gut is
a tapeworm gorging
on fetid air.

Hiroshima

The floating feeling
of walking on air on
intricately woven tightropes

to the peace park,
re-sown from scratch, well-groomed,
with a few choice plaques

and little need for words,
just a few mushrooms sprouting
by the tree trunks, and under benches.

The pink hair and converse boots,
berets and badges distinguish
the two American expats

from the rest of the youths.
Kids in their own backyard,
they skateboard the park's paths

as if in a dream world,
oblivious to pedestrians
and the tightness of corners,

the dangerous curves intimating
they'd crash at their own peril.
The Scalectrix scream of wheels on gravel.

The Chair

It takes five men to strap him in,
like a child on a dodgem.
The first makes a casket of the ankles,

the second pins a strap across the chest.
The third, a priest, intones whilst
anointing the ears with Vaseline.

The fourth, the administrator, ensures
no risk of whiplash, crosschecks the eyes
for crusts of sleep, instructs a fifth man

inserting the bit, like a large prawn cracker
or holy wafer, abundant with ridges
to stop the sixth biting off

his tongue. As the lampshade is lowered,
his limbs are so heavy, no man
need check he is earthed.

Dead Poets' Society

'O Captain, my Captain!'
Walt Whitman

The morning after
its first network screening,
our gowned Headmaster
delivered his assembly
in uncomfortably solemn tones.

So keen was he to quash
a groundswell of rebellion,
so driven to quell
the feared poetic uprising,
that his closing statement
was romanticism dissected,
and staged precisely
for a thousand strong jury.

It wasn't his style
to condemn outright
the underage drinking
and heady musings of
boys baying at the moon.

He didn't cite
the class split
into a *shipwreck of souls*,
some alighted on tables,
others, buttock clenched
to stool, in fear of the cane.

He warned us instead
of defying our parents,
half-baked ideals,
and the perils
of staying awake
after the watershed.

As he exited stage right,
his two-step
drowned out by
murmurs and jeers,
every single boy
remained in his seat.

Yet in hindsight
I am dismayed
at how easily
he may have prevailed
if, sobered by salaries,

we might later
have reneged upon rebellion,
forced into becoming
captains of industry
by his dark-robed
visions of guilt.

news from
back home

If you want to become whole,
let yourself be partial.
Tao Te Ching, Lao Tzu

Mook

Roused from dream,
her reflex is to latch,
to tug at your teat
like a clicking cub.

Her palate's too high,
or jaw too clamped,
so she cones it like a lipstick
until it's raw and red.

The pain makes you grit,
as excess milk drips,
and your aureola stings
as the blebs slowly heal,

so you coax her
to the other side
to ease your swollen duct.

Stranded from sleep,
our babe clung tight,
you wonder if
we're not doing it right,
if sharing the bed is daft

when elbows flail,
and pillows rumple,
and our snores are the sea,
and her ear is a conch.

For tonight she seems
to writhe too much,
to rouse too soon,
and plunge too fast
into the cushion
of your yielding chest.

Docking for an hour to suck,
she curls in on top,
her foetal tuck so heavy that
your ribs seem to creak.

You're shut out from dreams,
damp and cross, and
your nipple's the key
bent in the teeth of the lock.

First words

When you say *zszshuuh*
I imagine you see
the bee extend
its aura into
lovely lavender

When you say *up-down*
I see arms rise and,
as you fold your knees,
your *bo-tt-om* dives
into the duvet

When you say *mum-mum*
I imagine no
comma between
your mouth her nipple
and the heartbeat of the poplar

Things I Never Knew

for our first born

That I could assume the guise of a throne,
and my lap yield like memory foam,
moulding to your tailbone
every time you squirm.

That I'd be as staunch as a tree
swaying parabolas in the dark,
rocking you to drowsiness
as the lullabies loop,
and my creaky knees waltz
over toes splayed like roots.

That I'd be a bird,
my veganism deferred
as I pull meat from the bone,
regurgitate it as mush
on my finger spoon,
knowing you may demur,
as it slides down your cheeks
to dollop on the floor.

That I'd cameo as a swing,
my rusty frame strained,
my hands firm about your ribs,
as the pendulum that's you
oscillates over the fulcrum of my abs,
and we're giddy
as the world is flung from its axis.

That I could endlessly relive the thrill
of the flip and catch, certain I will
never let you drop,
for your heartbeat resounds
as clearly as a clapper
in the cupped bell of my palms.

Omen

1

Scritch scratch, scrabbled the bird in the shaft,
as stricken as a murmur in the chimney's clay heart.

Crick crick. Wing scraped brick,
powerless to undo its plummet into dark.

A dozy pigeon, we supposed,
had blundered into this sarcophagus,

so we sat in witness, exiled on
the brink of breath,

until the *shlip shlap* of its sometimes flap
broke off.

And our sighs stretched to fill the gap,
as if somehow they might resuscitate,

but we'd deduced by then that death
was set to cameo in our lives.

2

Beeep. I spoke to a machine, alerting the sanctuary just in case,
and rehearsed ferrying the bird's sack of lung and bones

in a straw-lined box
we'd puncturedwith a bradawl-
pfff pfff- to make air vents.

We lowered the mirror in case
a phoenix emerged, and smashed its beak,
drawn to the illusion of space.

Then we steeled ourselves for a scene of frail wings,
removed the stove
and lowered the sooty flue.

Casual crumbs trickled, *csshhcsshh*
kicking up charcoal,
but no loosening debris rustled.

So we left the room to regain its composure.

3

Minutes passed, then
I heard the thud of floorboards,
as its body, flung at the window,

rebounded *thump thump*
in a sprawling heap.

I rushed in for proof of an afterlife,
only to glimpse the bird blur

into the garden through
the gape of the outstretched door –
a starling perhaps, though I can't be sure,

its discreet *plip plop* betraying
but a creamy smear,
caking on the window sill.

Blackberries

…the satisfying pluck
from the torus, its
pleasant pop, ping
and rebound between

the lever of finger
and thumb. Crushed juice
on the tongue is tainted
by the wire-thin pain

of microscopic thorns,
but we don't notice
as we tingle and tang
to our heart's content.

How strange that
your patient designs
for crumble and custard
contrast so sharply with mine:

to waltz through hedgerows,
spit out mould, ravage every
membrane and lap up the syrup
from every cleft, dark and down…

Concrete

We've lugged these paving slabs twenty feet, and shunted them onto plastic sheets. Dad's catching his breath, ready to wax strategical on how to mix the cement.

I secretly suck my grazed knuckles as I digest his plan, and press thumbs into my swollen lumbar, as if to lube its seized-up hinge,

then stoop to shovel *five-ten-fifteen* non-stop loads from the jumbo bag of ballast into this rickety barrow. My biceps bite, my glutes grip.

I inch towards the slabs, as my knees teeter and the dry axle screeches. I huff and rasp, wheeze and puff, pronate my fists and push the handles skywards to unload the slop.

With his mattock, Dad folds in the gypsum, forms a well in its darkened flour, tipping in rain from the barrel, as he works the rugged dough into a coarse slurry.

I hear it slurp as I scrape it up, with my spade as straight as a bayonet. I pigeon step towards the trench, with my deltoids like guy ropes strung tightly to my spine.

I watch how he nudges and kneads, then smooths the mix into every crevice, with this painstaking method he's loathe to share, no matter how fatigued.

Slumped from the strain, I imagine we might one day make these foundations from springy bread, our hierarchy upset, for nursing the yeast would surpass his expertise.

Palette

Melanin mud: use in porches, to disguise splotchy boots, soggy leaves, snotty rags.

Samphire swash: designed for nurseries, for parents aspiring to underwater frescoes.

Sepia swoon: conceived for spacious hallways. Complements the *rosy tint* range, e.g. *retro ruby, souvenir sunset, throwback teak*.

Mystic mould: apply sparingly in utility spaces. May intensify washing machine hypnosis, or soften tedium by tumble dryer. Can bring on epiphany in the eaves.

Maudlin mauve: ideal for dusty libraries, especially of romantic verse.

Bastard black: depth-defying. Will indulge all visions of escape.

White warp: recommended for filling cracks in plaster, fissures in skirting, or dangerous splits in the seams of your soul.

Tabula Rasa

for Phap Linh

These clumps of hair I've clipped
cartwheel across the sandstone.
Catharsis begun, I go in to inspect
my chocolate scalp in the sunlit bathroom.

I stare at the flecks of salt and pepper,
and dandruff clung to the grain.
I want to erase dead thoughts,
reboot to zero, let the wind rush in.

I apply this meringue of lathered foam,
then click a new blade into the sleek, metallic razor.
Shorn of specs, I turn and squint
into this hand-held looking glass.

Swiping in this maze of mirrors,
I snag no skin and draw no blood,
leaving microscopic roots in the gleam
of the newly smoothed surface.

My melanin crown brings to mind
the day you were ordained:
the monk's ceremonial cleansing
when three nuns stooped
to shave your stubbled pate.

Soothed by their airy touch, your pale dome
glowed in the flash of clicking phones,
as your eyelids were half-closed, poised
like magnolia petals at dusk.

To soften this frown here in my solitary reflection,
to trust myself enough that I embrace all beings,
is to be as unfazed as you were that day,
by the camera crew's scrum,

the brush of their furry mic,
and the orange embers
collapsing through the giant skylights.

Acts of Plumbing Kindness

1

Thanks for the time
you tiptoed to the *en suite*
in holey black socks,
and deftly replaced
the cistern's float rod and ballcock,
muttering *fudge* when
the spilled spanner clinked,
for my daughter was snoozing snugly
on my chest.

2

Huddled under duvets
one foggy Friday night,
we're glad when you emerge
to mend the filling loop's
broken tap.
A five minute job.
A twenty minute chat.
Chipper old flirt, with eyeliner
as dark as stout,
you can't stem the flow
of anecdotes, regaling us
with your light-lisped gospel,
in which a child comes first.
How they must have feted
your first born,
before you traipsed home
along the train tracks,
hours after the lock-in,
heady on microbrew and stars.

3

You swig the dregs of tea,
slip on your tatty boots,
leave to resurrect
a clapped-out boiler.
As you waggle torchlight
through the back doors
of your dented van,
we catch the peep show
of u-bends in p-traps,
and funnels in tubes,
and there in the legroom
of the passenger's seat
your full-bodied stash
of pinots and plonks:
the legacy of your refusal
to take cash.

4

Dad recalls that first job
when you lugged away asbestos,
and tipped the storage heaters.

Rushing to plumb the loo,
you slipped,
piercing your scalp
on a light bulb's shards.

Woozy, you refused
Dad's offer to drive,
and chugged to A and E
with blood oozing
through makeshift gauze
onto your steering wheel.

Dad recalls watching you
from the doorway,
o so dumbstruck
that he sobbed.

Spheres

for Amber

We've watched these bubbles
float away, or fall, then

rainbow burst and fade
on the sandstone floor.

My delighted daughter pleads for *more.*
So I restart this show,

exhaling spheres
like startled clouds

whose glycerine tangents
kiss fleetingly.

She chases each one with outstretched arms,
certain she'll possess it
like a snowstorm globe,

but they break on her fingertips
a hundred single times.

And her amnesia's
a trigger
for impetuous joy.

A resurgent breeze swoops in
before my pursed lips unlock.

A flurry of miniature suns flow,
and their orbits glint,

as they mimic
a drift of dandelion clocks.

Post-op

Dad propped you up
like a marionette,
locked his arms
under you neck,
and levering his elbows
on the edge of the sink,
ensured you were angled
so as not to choke.

The air nudged out
from your lungs
in steady rasps
and when all was clear
you wheezed to project
some alien expulsion,
a stark, spinachy concoction
I'd never imagined within.

Your eyes were askew,
dad's straight ahead.
His ear, close in
on your back,
seemed to stethoscope
what remained of
breakfast and breath.

a word from our sponsor, mother earth

Rêveur, j'en sentirai la fraîcheur à mes pieds,
Je laisserai le vent baigner ma tête nue.
Arthur Rimbaud

Knole

There are
quiet spots
the deer vacate,

and to sit tight,
eyes shut,
is to absorb

the footfalls
of their
curious comeback,

to sit in
goose-bumped shade,
acorns lining tusk-like roots,

sometime slivers of sunset
etching redcurrant
onto eyelids,

is to see
the world tilt
between archives of the breath.

Culpeper's Witness

and is especial good for ruptures and broken bones;
yea, it is said to be so powerful… that, if they
are boiled with dissevered pieces of flesh in a pot,
it will join them together again.
Nicholas Culpeper, *Culpeper's Complete Herbal*

1

To this musty place I was dragged,
blindfolded and gagged,
their fists as snug as manacles
on my shattered wrist.

A terse voice bid these henchmen
to shunt me inches from a roaring hearth.
Welcome, he barked.

There I knelt and spluttered
until a boiling broth shot up,
and singed my clammy brow.

I yelped, wailed and pled,
until they tore away my blindness.
My eyes ached in the crepuscule,
focusing with haste on a cauldron,

the rolling blackness within
as thick and glistening
as the devil's haemorrhage.

Knitbone, they said. Recoiling from
its wretched stink, I struggled
not to spew my morning's victuals.

Behold, he declaimed, as his brutes
threw a butchered hen
into the pitch black meniscus,

and what I saw next obeyed
the logic of no science in which
I am versed.

Unable to repeal their testimony,
my eyes must attest to its truth.

2

Dead bird's wings lurch with a crunch into capsized chest. Neck snaps back into place, fuses with the crown of the bobbing breast-skin hangs pink and flaccid. Immaculate callipers of blunted bone rebound off the slackened chest, as relentless clots fleck like crushed garnet. Half-splayed thighs draw into the carcass with a sallow slurp, and the slippery ease of such integration shocks my brain like a gavel. O how the gizzard, liver, limbs merge with precision, and the wishbone claws arise from the copper-bottomed depths.

3

When I awake, shivering on this nowhere hill,
my broken joint somehow fixed,
and the comfrey and chicken still acrid on my lips,

I recall this macabre vision that shall scar my convalescence.

O dear Lord smite this indelible image,
and reveal to whom I should pray
to heal me from this dream

in which sluggish bones weld,
flesh hangs in ragged vermillion
and I reek of bilious leaf.

Early Recordings

I clutch at the scutch,
peek out from sedge
at the needle's skittery hop,

as it engraves peep and
tweet, twitter and *psssiii*:
birdsong striking into vinyl

as warblers' scratch,
wrens' scrambly gossip,
magpies' rattle-prattle.

I rise to retrieve the turn-
table, back to my study,
shutting out farm sounds

for earnest, confined days,
head down to transcribe
the trills, annotating staves

with never-before-seen
hieroglyphs, for which
I'm inventing the key.

Unpicking the woodcocks'
landed claims, I still find music
of leisurely longing, or alleluias

piping early at the sun's door,
then the universal screeching *seeeee*
as a hawk stalks above, soaring

over quickly hushed canopies,
before the starlings pipe up,
bristle with matey *hut-tah–dahs,*

then taunting the ornithologists
with *yerdunno-fukof-leeeeeeeve,*
cheer in descant *teehee tewits teehee.*

Beeline

When the engineer pins
the bee's wing
to a blueprint,
delves and rips
into its secrets,

and Faust-like,
trades knowledge
of the light-stitched-
pluck-tough surface

to a conglomerate,
hell-bent on patents
for body armour
and flying machines;

When the hives
lie abandoned,
their keepers
now guardians
of rotten honeycomb,

their poignant pleas
lost in the knowledge
that the transmitter
deflected them off course;

When winds and
unskilled hands
scatter the pollen,
and the orchards
lie barren and

high street bosses
rue the shortage of
apples and honey,
almonds and cotton;

When the queen
abdicates her
brood chamber,
sick and sorrowed
by starvation,

stops to hang
in a hollow tree,
her solitude
a slow dying;

When the scent
of anise and pheromones
can't call them back,
as if they've homed in
on some God given

*Do any
of us know
where they're
headed?*

First Night

Lightning erupts:
The floodlit sky is
a million strobes bright.

Stars tread soft
not to be heard

over the drilling crickets,
and Dylan's waltz
tinkling from the heights.

Souillac

To shape to plunge,
feint and then glide
in this rush hour of swallows,
perform swooped eights
on the warm currents
outside the cloister,
as our hairs stand up on end.

Into the fray, precocious
and sleek, enters an albino
who cannot escape
the burden of colour,
and is tracked and stalked.
Never is the chase frantic,
as fatal as breakneck

or the skim of bullets,
although one expects
blood to speck quicker
than the eye can see,
on tenterhooks as
beak stabs breast,
and talons tumble from the sky.

Nuit Blanche

The mosquitoes'
kamikaze turn

and the wasps'
drumming dawn

through invisible windows
awaken you.

Dazed by midges,
your sweat a metallic coat,

a lacquer of
teeming rivulets,

you hear wood doves wheezing,
coo-cooing midnight

like a grandfather clock warbling
its drawn-out semantics;

Their wings beat fleshily,
thumping at the leaves

with the disdain of branches.
The night propels

its black blood
into the loam, but the dawn

is wet and withdrawn
like a lover, mid-dream, playing solitaire...

Three Haiku

Slow, orange embers
counsel the young, eager flames
– *long evening whisper*

***

Beleaguered in snow,
I cannot trust your footprints
without knowing why

***

Having mastered the
secrets of surface tension
Jesus walked and talked

***

Wheal Coates

Beyond the plummet of this rock world,
even the scree has taken on russet,
taken on evening, only to lose it.

We are rich here, could fill a knapsack,
if we wanted, with the bell heather
or yellow gorse that blankets the headland.

Ferns line the path like lilac
caterpillars, curling into a crisp.
The ruins, jutting out

their Cubist vision, are watchful.
You can read vigilance in the slats
of the meurtrières, adorned as they are

with greying blackbirds. From such
silence, it seems only the sea itself
is squawking. Gulls overhang

as cormorants splice the sea
into a patchwork of lanterns.
Seeing men climb the rock-face

a dog yelps suddenly in the dusk.

Happy

for Emma

Because the first piping cuppa hits the spot,
and breakfast is a wagon wheel
of eggy bread and apple slice.

Because plucking her Satsuma
clean of its whiskers,
its tangle of pith clings to my tongue.

Because on our walk a huntsman doffs his hat
as the fox cub in my rucksack
is alert and surreptitious.

Because the lilac plums are plush
and untouched by wasps,
and their juices make us heady;

Because we laugh in the overgrown grass,
about ventriloquists throwing farts,
and gorge on just-baked bread, dipped in rhubarb pulp;

Because we nap in the hammock until
the postman delivers bills
we lovingly shred for compost;

Because we pedal to the hilltop
to catch the sunset,
and the sweat dries off
as we freewheel back;

Because we owe our girls
a happy landing
before we fade to black.

Acknowledgements

Thanks to the editors of the following publications in which earlier versions of some of these poems first appeared: *Acumen, Agenda Broadsheet 7*, *Bedford Square 4*, *Haiku Scotland, The Interpreter's House, Magma, The North, Poetry Review, Poetry Wales, The Rialto* and *Stand*.

Many thanks to the following for their input and feedback: Nicholas Menon, Andrew Motion, Jo Shapcott and, of course, Emma.